LIMIT
YOURSELF
AND UNLEASH YOUR
CREATIVITY!

LAURENCE KING

Published in 2019 by
Laurence King Publishing Ltd
361–373 City Road
London EC1V 1LR
United Kingdom
www.laurenceking.com

A catalogue record for this book is available from the British Library.

ISBN: 978-1-78627-503-5

Typeset in Gravur Condensed & Eames Century Modern

Printed in China

Laurence King Publishing is committed to ethical and sustainable
production. We are proud participants in The Book Chain Project®
bookchainproject.com

Ralph Burkhardt

LIMIT YOURSELF AND UNLEASH YOUR CREATIVITY!

Laurence King Publishing

TABLE OF CONTENTS

01 LIMITATIONS OF TIME

02 LIMITATIONS OF RESOURCES

03 LIMITATIONS OF DESIGN PRINCIPLES

04 LIMITATIONS OF A BRIEF

05 LIMITATIONS OF MEDIUM

06 LIMITATIONS OF SKILLS

07 LIMITATIONS OF SPACE

FINAL THOUGHTS

WHAT, WHY, WHO?

I first stumbled on the topic of 'limitations' when I was invited overseas to give a lecture to graphic design students. What I didn't want was to deliver another 'skip-through-my-portfolio' presentation. Usually, people already know your work from the Internet; that's why they invited you. I wanted to give them something new, something interesting, something to take away.

So I thought to myself: 'What can I share with these students? What is a situation we all have to deal with in our creative life, especially when we are young and inexperienced?' I tried to remember being a student myself, and what I hated the most was being given exercises with no restrictions at all. I would have no clue where to start or what materials to use. I knew I couldn't illustrate well and that I was always interested in typography, so I focused on my strength. Back then, I somehow lived with my limitations and accepted them as my burden.

Until recently, I did not have an awareness of how limitations are embedded in almost every aspect of my life, not just my creative life.

I was never a big fan of 'how-to' books, but the issue of limitations is too important not to address. Every day, creatives struggle with restrictions, and the omnipresent myth that freedom is liberating, or even necessary to keep creativity alive. In this book, you will find out why this is completely wrong!

Limit Yourself will show you that limitations are nothing to fear. On the contrary, they can be very stimulating. This pocket companion will help you to define your limitations, show you how to deal with them and stimulate you to become a truly creative problem-solver.

Keep this book close to your work desk for inspiration, and whenever you feel limited or stuck, remind yourself that you are not the only one dealing with limitations.

Ralph Burkhardt

'I DON'T REMEMBER EVER BEING FORCED TO ACCEPT COMPROMISES, BUT I HAVE WILLINGLY ACCEPTED CONSTRAINTS.'

Charles Eames

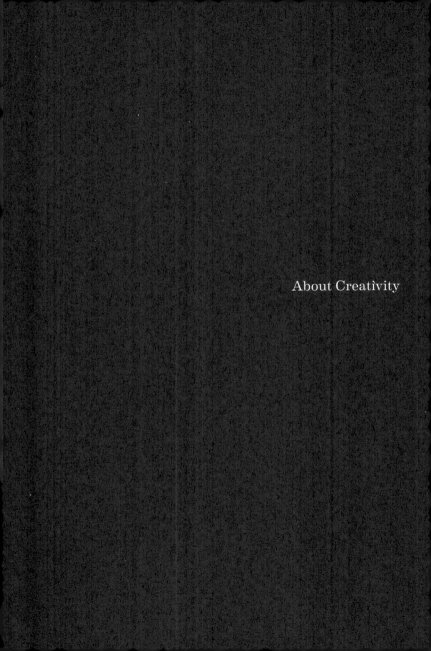

About Creativity

WHAT IS CREATIVITY?

In brief, creativity is the ability to create something 'new and useful'. Although creativity is not measurable like IQ, it is one of the most important characteristics of being human.

The most obvious difference between intelligence and creativity is that intelligence requires convergent thinking, which means the ability to give a single right answer to a standard question. Creativity requires divergent thinking in order to come up with as many potential answers as possible.

That's why creative people realize that every experience is potentially valuable. They are more open to new ideas and experiences, and pay attention to seemingly minor details.

Of course we all have ideas, but to make them see the light of day is what really makes you creative – everything else is just imaginative. Creativity demands all of your persistence, and forces you to get out of your comfort zone, to fail and to get up again.

EVERYONE CAN BE CREATIVE!

Creativity is no longer seen as something that only artists or so-called 'creatives' possess. It is not an inborn talent that some people have and others don't. People who don't believe they are creative tend to avoid situations where they need to be creative to succeed. This is often due to their perception of what creativity is.

Let me tell you something: creativity is a skill for everyone to learn! It's important to know that we are all born naturally creative, but that a surfeit of rules and regulations make us learn to be uncreative.

We need somehow to preserve our inner child. Children can easily get lost in their imagination and daydreaming, and don't care about imperfection or being realistic. That is what makes them so light-hearted and creative. Instead of balancing the pros and cons, children simply jump in.

Great minds say that all these attributes are key to creativity.

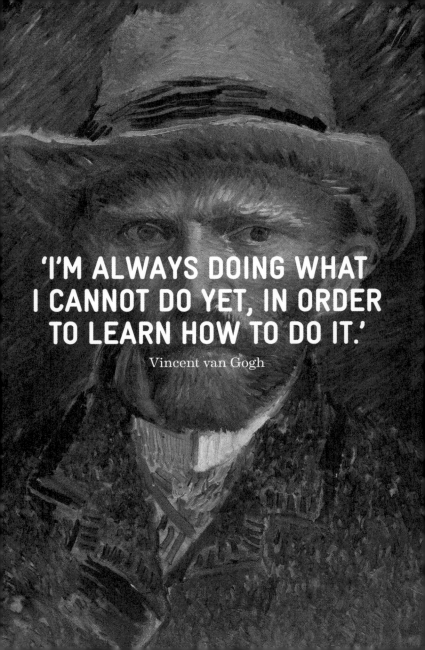

'I'M ALWAYS DOING WHAT
I CANNOT DO YET, IN ORDER
TO LEARN HOW TO DO IT.'

Vincent van Gogh

THE TRUE CREATIVE MYTH

Creativity can be learned, practised and used in the same way as, say, mathematics. Some will be more adept at being creative than others, but it is definitely possible to gain a reasonable level of competence.

When we talk about creativity, the myth of a muse's kiss is still deeply rooted in most people's perception. Well, there are certainly some 'Aha!' moments in finding ideas, especially when you distract yourself and don't think about it too much. However, these moments are rare, and most of the time creativity is hard work – only the best know how to make it look frustratingly easy.

To be creative, all you need is the courage to experiment, the persistence to ask questions, the open-mindedness to network, the desire to explore, and the courage to deal with limitations. You have all of that? Perfect, then the magic formula is ...

THE CREATIVE PROCESS

... to copy, to connect and to transform!

First, realize that every new idea is just a copy of something that already existed – nothing is born out of nothing. Just go out there and start to copy everything you see. Make it yours!

The next step is to make connections between seemingly unrelated things. To make these connections, soak up everything you can, as it might be useful one day. Be curious! With a broad knowledge base, a creative person can make a wider range of connections. Set up an archive full of pictures, colours, magazines, books, etc. Let's call it your 'visual mood board' that you can always refer to.

The last step is to transform your visual collection: mash things up, remix, change colours and forms, minimize, maximize, exaggerate, elaborate, contrast, intensify, simplify ...

COPY
CONNECT
TRANSfØRM

REFLECT ON YOUR CREATIVITY

Some years ago, I was asked to write a comprehensive manual about graphic design. At first I was hesitant about the huge amount of research I faced, but knowing there is rarely a second chance, I accepted the challenge.

I was really glad I did, because it forced me to think about what I am actually doing all day long. It helped me to organize my thoughts and intentions about graphic design, and in the process I learned a lot about myself and my attitude as a designer. It felt like going to school again. It made me question why I did things in a specific way and gave me confidence in looking for new creative paths.

I recommend that every creative practises their writing skills. After all, a great idea is only a great idea once you've shared it with the world.

☛ Write three paragraphs about yourself, what excites you and why you do the job you do. It will help keep you motivated and on the right creative track.

THINK INSIDE THE BOX

Thinking 'outside the box' is an expression that is inseparably connected to creativity, suggesting that we need to escape from the straitjacket of rules if we are to reinvent the world.

In my opinion, the metaphor 'to think outside the box' is misleading. There is no need to escape the box. On the contrary, creatives need a box to know what boundaries to push against. The box is a starting point that makes it possible to see what we have to work with and how our ideas can grow and expand from there.

What would creative thought be like without a box? Faced with endless possibilities, no walls to climb, no boundaries to push – indeed, no pressure at all – you would lose the urge to search for solutions.

So embrace the box if you want to think outside it!

THIS SIDE UP

'THE MORE NOBLE THE ENDEAVOUR, THE MORE, IN A WAY, THE CONSTRAINT GOES AWAY.'

Yves Béhar

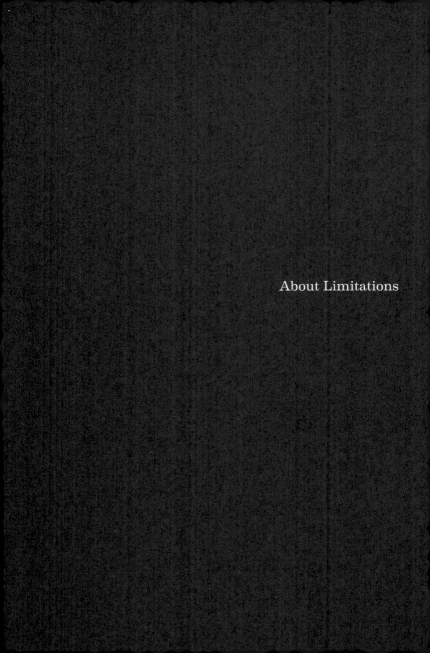

About Limitations

'LIMITATION' MIGHT SOUND LIKE A BAD WORD

✘ Limitations are something you can't do.

✘ They restrict what you're allowed to do.

✘ Limitations take away freedom.

✘ They remove options.

✘ Limitations are rules *you* didn't set.

limitation

/ˌlɪmɪˈteɪʃ(ə)n/

[1] A limiting rule or circumstance: a restriction.
[2] The action of limiting something. *

WHO NEEDS LIMITATIONS?

We all do! Every move we make, every solution we think of is restricted by a number of limitations. Limitations are all around us. They help us with solving problems and make us question everything about our work and life.

Working within limitations is not solely reserved for artists or designers. Most people, from engineers to editors, have to overcome creative obstacles. A lot of people just don't know what their limitations are or how stimulating limitations can be.

First of all, we have to separate the two kinds of limitations:

Limitations imposed by others, such as clients.

Limitations imposed by ourselves, such as working with a limited colour palette.

'THE GREATEST FREEDOM
COMES FROM THE
GREATEST STRICTNESS.'

Paul Valéry

WHAT KIND OF LIMITATIONS ARE THERE?

▸ Commercial limitations
such as time.

▸ Limitations on resources
such as budget or working material.

▸ Design principles
such as 'form follows function'.

▸ Requirements
such as from a briefing.

▸ Limitations of medium
such as technical requirements.

▸ Skills
such as drawing, which we may or may not do well.

▸ Limitations of space
such as a tiny work area.

WHEN LIFE GIVES YOU LEMONS … [SEE PAGE 47]

* The Juicy Salif, Philippe Starck's not-so-functional lemon squeezer
for Alessi.

WHAT LIMITATIONS CAN DO FOR YOU

Our brain is constantly in efficiency mode, always looking for ways to use less energy. Quite often, unless forced, we don't think much at all. Limitations do the exact opposite – they force you to think. Limitations also inspire better thinking – thinking that challenges the status quo and encourages us to act more resourcefully.

Being limited is a bit like losing one of the five senses. The restriction immediately heightens your other senses. The same goes for your creative work. If you're restricted in one creative field – illustration, for example – this will push your creativity further in other disciplines, such as typography. The potential has always been there, but it takes a constraint in another area to push your skills to the fore.

☛ Draw a mind map of things you can or can't do. Once you know your limitations, you can start figuring out how to work with and around them successfully.

Limitations encourage us to:

‣ solve problems resourcefully.

‣ rethink how we define success and failure.

‣ frame our thinking.

‣ gain focus in a world of constant distraction.

‣ be more efficient.

‣ find new ways of collaborating.

‣ create solutions in new and unexpected ways or places.

‣ reinvent ourselves.

‣ find ways to experiment and to take risks.

WHAT YOU NEED TO BRING

Attitude

Do you believe it is possible to turn limitations into possibilities? No? Then reframe your thinking: problem-solvers need positivity.

Ambition

How much do you want it? You need to be totally invested to come up with a groundbreaking solution.

Approach

Do you know how to start? Get out of your comfort zone and be prepared to confront obstacles head on!

WHAT YOU DON'T NEED TO BRING

Fear

Especially the fear of the blank page. Fail, fail again, fail better.

Faintheartedness

Be bold! Be ambitious! Only the brave will change the world.

Freedom

Total freedom doesn't inspire at all. Total freedom limits, while limitations liberate!

WHEN WORK BEGINS THIS:

WE ALL START WITH

WHO'S AFRAID OF THE BLANK PAGE?

Every creative artist! We all know the fear of the blank page, screen or canvas staring directly at us.

When every option is in front of you, it's difficult to decide what to do. It's too soon to know which idea will be good and which will be less successful.

We prefer instead to stay in our safe zone, where we can avoid the anxieties that go along with the uncertainty of choosing. There is no reason not to start, though. Our first creative moves are pretty random anyway, so why not start with defining some limitations? They will take the responsibility of making early arbitrary decisions off our shoulders and let us start creating immediately.

Imagine painting a picture. Let's say you limit your palette to just three colours:

you can start with a warm red. then add green next to it and continue with yellow. Each successive brushstroke after the red will be less and less arbitrary (and daunting) than the ones before because you will have a better sense of how the colours work together. A picture will emerge, and suddenly you'll have begun to create.

THE CREATIVE TRAJECTORY

work begins

Don't care at all...

Panic!

deadline

work

work

work

while

crying

41

WHY TOTAL FREEDOM DOESN'T LIBERATE

When we talk about the creative process, we think of a free and limitless environment. It's easy to see total freedom and unlimited means as the only way to achieve cutting edge ideas and breakthrough innovations.

The opposite is true: it sounds like a paradox, but total freedom limits, while limitations liberate. Working within a restrictive environment is calming for most creatives. It feels like not having total control over a situation can actually set you free.

But how is it that total freedom and lack of any structure or limitations result in paralysis? In many cases, this has to do with a particular form of pressure: the pressure of choice.

In psychology, the phenomenon is known as 'The tyranny of choice'. Studies show that the more choices you have, the more difficult it becomes to make a decision.

If we make a choice, how can we be sure this is the right one or the best one? We end up preferring not to make a choice at all. In our mind, choosing becomes losing, and this is something we want to avoid at all cost.

Too many choices limit creativity, as does having no choice at all.

CREATIVE BOUNDARIES

How is it that having a boundary makes you more liberated in creative terms?

Researchers use the analogy of a playground to explain the phenomenon.

When you put a fence around a playground, children will explore the whole space because they feel safe to play all the way to the edges. They know that the fence will keep them from going astray, and they play more freely with that boundary in place. Once you remove the fence, the children tend to stay in the middle. They might explore a little bit, but they mainly stay close together where it's 'safe'.

The same happens in the creative process: having no limitations means we are not sure what territory to explore and what walls to push against. We lose focus of the problem we are meant to be solving. We need boundaries to explore closer to the edge creatively and to push the limits.

READY, MINDSET, GO!

Creativity has a lot do with the right mindset and persistence. Adopting a positive attitude naturally results in creativity.

Think of a challenge that you could easily succeed in. Now impose a limitation on yourself, such as having to reach that goal within a certain timeframe or with half the budget. To overcome the restriction of a limitation, you have to set up a positive mindset to succeed.

'Do I believe it is possible?' is an important question when dealing with limitations. If you are optimistic about this question, or if you have already dealt successfully with limitations, you will embrace any restrictions, no matter what. Inspiration is also very important. What others have already achieved will encourage you to do the same.

The optimism gained from having turned a limitation into a possibility gives you the confidence to do it again. You also start to learn the process of getting things going. It's like lifting weights: it strengthens the creative muscles.

You know you can do it, and each time you do it, it becomes easier. You will become a true problem-solver and will start to see offers everywhere.

To quote a popular saying, 'When life gives you lemons, make lemonade.'

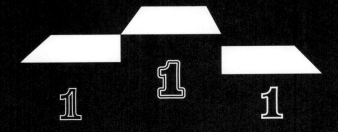

'IF I AM LOOKING FOR AN IDEA, I USUALLY GIVE MYSELF A VERY SHORT TIME TO WORK ON IT [...] I FIND IT DIFFICULT TO ACTUALLY THINK FOR HOURS, BUT 30 MINUTES I CAN MANAGE.'

Stefan Sagmeister

Limitations of Time

01

LEARN TO LOVE DEADLINES

Cutting back on the time you have available for a project is probably pretty scary for most creatives. Deadlines are definitely not fun, but they help you. They force you to focus and prevent you from getting distracted.

We all waste too much time trying to figure out where to start. Limitations give us that time back by focusing what time we have, and forcing us to take a hard look at what's really important for our project.

Steve Jobs, the late co-founder of Apple, was notorious for setting 'impossible deadlines' aimed at bringing out the best, most creative energy in his employees. He famously gave software engineers just two weeks to outline their software vision for the first iPhone.

By limiting your time, you're telling your mind to focus and fully engage, even if it's just for a short burst. Your approach to work changes dramatically when you have a one-day deadline. Don't overdo it, though: giving yourself one day to write a book is a recipe for disaster.

Robert Bresson

'EXPRESSION
THROUGH
COMPRESSION.'

MAKE BETTER USE OF YOUR TIME

Time is a valuable resource. We all have the feeling we are running out of time, despite all of our little digital helpers, which should give us more time. How is this possible? It's mainly because of distraction.

First of all, put your smartphone away, don't let Siri grab your attention and don't do 99 other things while reading this paragraph. Although multitasking makes us feel productive, the truth is our brains just can't handle it.

Our average attention span is eight seconds! We are not programmed to think about more than one thing at a time. In fact, we manage about 50 per cent less when attempting to multitask.

In other words, try single-tasking for greater productivity. That way you have to prioritize what the most important task is. For maximum impact always aim to be fully engaged in a task.

Here's how you can use your time to maximize your creativity:

☞ Create a disturbance-free work environment. Clean up your desk, for example.

☞ Structure your time, even your free time. It will give you more direction and purpose.

☞ Track your time to discover how you can make better use of it. It also helps to plan your budget for a certain project.

☞ Slow down and your actions will become more meaningful.

☞ If you are overwhelmed by the size of a problem, break it down into many bite-sized pieces.

☞ Set up goals. When you reach a goal in a defined time period, you start to feel successful. This motivates you to keep going.

☞ Take a break from time to time. It will reboot your brain and kick-start your creative thinking.

☞ Do less! When you do fewer things, you do them better.

THE FIVE-MINUTE TIME LIMIT

Dr Edward de Bono is a Maltese psychologist, philosopher and author. In his book *De Bono's Thinking Course,* he shares the idea of Five-Minute Thinking.

1 Minute ☞ Target and Task
First identify your target and task. The target is the desired outcome or focus of the thinking. The task is how you are going to reach your target.

2 Minutes ☞ Expand and Explore
In this part of the exercise, write down any ideas that come to mind. Try not to be critical or judgemental. According to de Bono, you're 'opening up the field, filling in the map, exploring the territory.'

2 Minutes ☞ Contract and Conclude
This is where you zero in on the problem and its solution. Try to make sense of your ideas. Test them out by balancing pros and cons.

Don't spend more than five minutes in total on these steps. By limiting your time, you're conditioning your mind to focus and fully engage.

'LIMIT GIVES FORM TO THE LIMITLESS.'

Pythagoras

ONE PAINTING/ POSTER/LOGO/ LETTERING A DAY

You have probably heard of the 'Painting a Day' phenomenon on social media, with all of its spin-offs – 'Poster a Day', 'Logo a Day', 'Lettering a Day'. It is a pure statement of limitation. There must be one painting per day, period.

The enthusiasm with which young artists and designers are partaking in this movement demonstrates their hunger for guidelines and organization.

After all, you can't rebel against such a clear instruction, can you? You have to do it. Perhaps that is what makes it such an important movement. It's not only about creating something within a day, it's about not waiting.

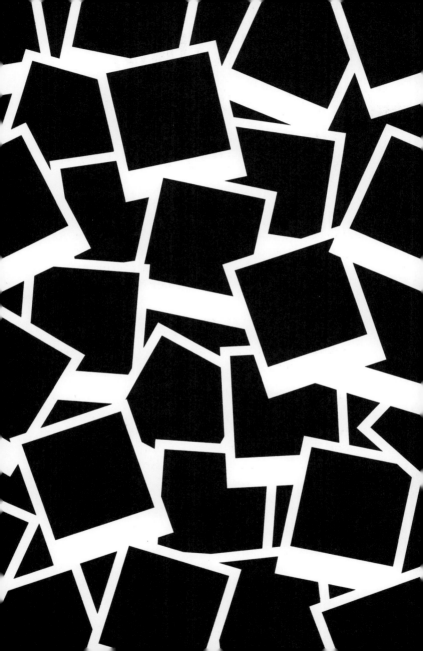

'I DON'T THINK OF TIME,
BUDGET, MATERIALS,
RAIN OR GRAVITY
AS LIMITATIONS, BUT
AS OPPORTUNITIES.'

Allan Wexler

Limitations of Resources

HOW TO DEAL WITH A LIMITED BUDGET

The golden days are over, and most companies have to deal with a limited budget – if not their own, then their consumer's. In such a climate, the new currency is not money, but creativity.

IKEA, for example, is known for its affordable and practical furniture. It starts with a price that the consumer is willing to pay and then works backwards to figure out a way to make it for that price. This is completely different from the approach of most other companies, which is what makes the IKEA ideology so special.

Ingvar Kamprad, the founder of IKEA, is famous for constantly asking questions about how the company can be improved. Which production process could be skipped or what costs could be lowered or eliminated? How could you make the product more ecologically safe or more durable and reliable?

'Making expensive things is easy,' Kamprad famously stated. 'Making affordable things that also work and last – that's the real challenge.'

* Billy is a bookcase developed in 1979 by Gillis Lundgren and IKEA.

IMPROVISATION = INNOVATION

Improvisation is a crude form of innovation. It is a spontaneous response, without any specific or scripted preparation, that forces us to go all out in the creative-thinking department. It can be a creative's best friend.

We are familiar with all kinds of improvisation used in music, acting or even in engineering. The Apollo 13 mission to the moon in April 1970 may be one of the most famous examples. After experiencing mechanical difficulties, the crew were forced to abandon their mission. Due to the damage that the spacecraft had endured, the astronauts had no choice but to move into the lunar module, which wasn't designed to hold three astronauts for as long as 96 hours, the time it would take to get them back to Earth. They quickly discovered that carbon dioxide was building up fast. With limited time and supplies, the astronauts managed to create an air filter by using one roll of grey duct tape, two liquid-cooled garment bags, two spacesuit hoses, two socks and one bungee cord.

The astronauts had nothing to lose, so they had to try things they normally wouldn't.

Opposite: The hack that saved the astronauts of *Apollo XIII*.

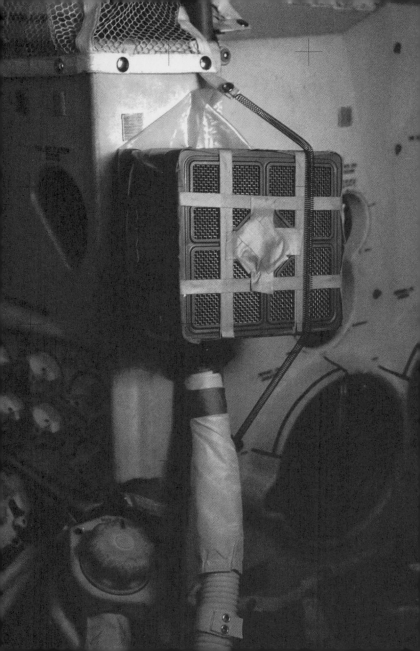

EXPLORATION THROUGH LIMITATION

The artist Allan Wexler is constantly exploring what is considered 'art', and self-imposed restrictions play a crucial part in his journey.

For his paintings, for instance, Wexler refrains from using professional art supplies and instead discovers functionality in conventional things. He makes colours from mustard, jam and ketchup; sheets of toilet paper soaked with milk become his working canvas; and a piece of a broomstick and a lock of hair form his paintbrush. By embracing self-inflicted restrictions in this way, Wexler allows new, more extreme creations to develop. As he puts it, he 'opens up new spaces within a world we thought we had defined'.

Experimental artists such as Wexler are genuinely resourceful. They have realized that self-imposed limitations force them to come up with answers that aren't the first and most obvious solution.

Opposite: For his architectural work, Wexler forced himself to live in very small spaces.

'GOOD DESIGN, LIKE GOOD PAINTING, COOKING, ARCHITECTURE OR WHATEVER YOU LIKE, IS A MANIFESTATION OF THE CAPACITY OF THE HUMAN SPIRIT TO TRANSCEND ITS LIMITATIONS.'

George Nelson

Limitations of Design Principles

REFINE YOUR COLOUR PALETTE

One of the easiest ways to spot an amateur designer is when they use every colour under the sun in a single piece. Reducing the number of colours used in a design actually makes the piece feel consistent. Think about some of the best exponents of graphic design: most, if not all, tend to use a small but vibrant palette for all of their designs. Some visual artists go even further. Yves Klein, for instance, is best known for his quest to find the perfect shade of blue. This fixation allowed him to explore the colour more fully, perfecting its use in his paintings and eventually leading him to patent his own shade, 'International Klein Blue'.

☛ Use the eyedropper tool in Photoshop to pick colours right out of a picture you are working with to make your design feel consistent.

☛ Make sure you have a range of values in your colour scheme. You will need some light and some dark colours to give contrast.

☛ There are colour schemes all around you! Look at nature, your bookshelf, or use a website for inspiration: https://color.adobe.com

PLEASE IMAGINE THE BLUEST BLUE

LIMIT YOUR TYPEFACES

Typography works in a similar way to colour, though perhaps on a more extreme scale. Using numerous fonts within a single design can become confusing and makes the layout look inconsistent. The human eye likes to settle into patterns of recognition, but using too many different typefaces can hinder this and interrupt the flow of reading.

Magazines and brochures can support a greater variety of typefaces than books and advertisements. But for most printed material two font families – one for headlines and titles, and one for body copy – are ample. Use bold, italics and different sizes of the font families for captions, subheadings and other design elements.

You can, of course, also limit yourself to only one typeface. German designer Mike Meiré, for instance, decided to work only with Helvetica for a whole decade. This is considered to be a neutral typeface without any intrinsic meaning in its form, so it allowed Meiré to focus on other elements on the page.

According to Massimo Vignelli, an Italian master of graphic design, there are only five typefaces you need. *

* Bodoni, Century, Futura, Helvetica, Times

WHY FRANK GEHRY LOVES LIMITATIONS

If you ask architect Frank Gehry, best known for creating the Guggenheim Museum in Bilbao and the Walt Disney Concert Hall in Los Angeles, what really inspires his work, he may give you an unexpected answer: 'Limitations'.

'It's better to have some problem to work on. I like to think we turn those constraints into action.'

It was, in fact, the strict standards for acoustics at the Walt Disney Concert Hall that led to Gehry's award-winning and unique design of the building's interior space. Designed as one large volume, the auditorium allows the occupants to be in the same space as the orchestra, creating impeccable acoustics within the hall. The façade was originally going to be limestone, but budget cutbacks and seismic-related worries forced Gehry to go with the panels of brushed stainless steel that have become iconic.

'YOU HAVE FREEDOM, SO YOU HAVE TO MAKE CHOICES – AND AT THE POINT WHEN I MAKE A CHOICE, THE BUILDING STARTS TO LOOK LIKE A FRANK GEHRY BUILDING. IT'S A SIGNATURE.'

Frank Gehry

MUSIC AT THE LIMITS

Limitations played a very important role for the Russian composer Igor Stravinsky (1882–1971). He loved to play around with musical composition by using self-imposed restrictions. In some works, for instance, he elected to use only certain pitches. He wrote: '... my freedom will be so much greater and more meaningful the more narrowly I limit my field of action, and the more I surround myself with obstacles.'

In pop music we also find musicians who restrict their possibilities to come up with more creative compositions. Peter Gabriel, for example, avoided using certain instruments. In his untitled album, often referred to as *Melt* (1980), he didn't use any cymbals, but relied on other percussion instruments.

'Artists given complete freedom die a horrible death,' Gabriel claims. 'So when you tell them what they can't do, they get creative and say, "Oh yes I can."' The album has been acclaimed as Gabriel's artistic breakthrough, establishing him as one of the most ambitious musicians.

Prince is another example of someone achieving more with less. His worldwide hit single 'When Doves Cry' has no bassline. No joke! Listen to it! In an unusual move for a dance song, he decided to leave the space unfilled. Prince said that there originally was a bassline but he thought it made the song sound too conventional and got rid of it.

All of these musicians embraced limitations to create something extraordinary.

'GIVE ME THE FREEDOM OF A TIGHT BRIEF.'

Unknown

Limitations of a Brief

'DO WHATEVER YOU LIKE!' the client said.

What a fabulous idea! Free to do whatever you want! Sounds like heaven – but it's problematic for creativity. Being completely free doesn't lead to quick answers and solutions. The result of a completely open brief is paralysation for most creatives because it is so easy to flounder and not know where to start.

When a client gives you restrictions right from the beginning, that's actually great as they are making a lot of the decisions for you. A specific brief facilitates an easier execution.

But the reality is that, most of the time, clients just don't know what they want or, sometimes, need. The result is a briefing with no restrictions. Having an open starting point makes it very difficult to find out what it is you're actually trying to solve. The best way to go from here is to debrief, or question, the client.

When debriefing, listen carefully, learn from the client and try to put yourself in their place. Empathy and asking the right questions lead to a clearer understanding of what is required.

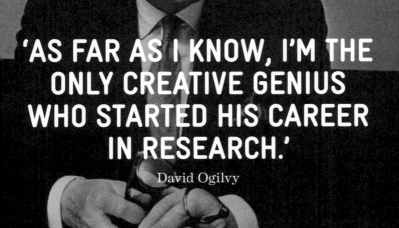

'AS FAR AS I KNOW, I'M THE ONLY CREATIVE GENIUS WHO STARTED HIS CAREER IN RESEARCH.'

David Ogilvy

DISCOVERING THE CLIENT'S NEEDS

If you want to come up with a creative solution, you need to ask the right questions. A question such as 'How can the client sell more products?' won't help you at all because it is too open-ended. To solve a problem you have to ask questions that contain the solution.

A more helpful question would be 'How can the client sell more products *without spending the whole budget*?' This sets a clear purpose but with a significant limitation that forces you to find ways other than conventional advertising to sell the product – perhaps through social media, for example.

It is the tension between purpose and limitation, no matter how paradoxical, that defines the task. Creativity is based on a paradoxical environment – it creates conflict, and this tension leads us to think in new ways.

Opposite: The interrobang is a punctuation mark combining question mark and exclamation mark. 'Creative questioning' proposes a question that contains an element of surprise.

Qualities of effective creative questioning:

▶ Ask a question that you've never asked before. It will need a completely different approach and forces you to leave your usual path and abandon all of your habitual thinking.

▶ Make sure your questions are specific, legitimate and challenging.

▶ Take the initiative in asking and answering 'paradoxical' questions.

▶ Remember, some of the most successful companies have got where they are by posing impossible questions for themselves.

▶ Constantly change the tenor of your questions. The same approach every time will lead you to the same outcome.

JUST DON'T DO IT

In the early 1980s Dan Wieden, co-founder of the US advertising agency Wieden + Kennedy, was confronted with some of the biggest limitations of his early career. How so? Nike's CEO Phil Knight had briefed him personally on developing a new brand campaign and made it very clear what he didn't want [SEE OPPOSITE].

When faced with this brief, Dan Wieden initially lowered his aspirations. All he knew was how to make great advertising, and all Nike wanted was no advertising at all. How could he make a compelling advertisement without the usual tools? But having to start from scratch took the pressure off. Triggered by this challenge, Wieden randomly found a picture of the Finnish Olympic runner Lasse Virén. He knew he needed to find a way to think like an athlete, so he tried to change perspective.

The first ad about the very nature of running wasn't stunning at all – but it didn't feel like conventional advertising and Nike liked it. So, from the seemingly unworkable beginning of having to deny everything he knew about advertising, Wieden came to believe his team could answer any impossible brief.

Opposite: Lasse Virén leads the Finland-Sweden athletics competition, 1980.

- **☒ NOTHING THAT LOOKS OR FEELS OR SMELLS LIKE 'ADVERTISING'**

- **☒ NEVER SHOW THE SAME AD TWICE**

- **☒ NO MODELS — DEFINITELY NO MODELS**

WHAT TO LEARN FROM DR. SEUSS

In May 1954, *Life* magazine blamed the fact that schoolchildren were not learning to read to a high enough standard on books being, frankly, boring. William Spaulding, the director of the education division at Houghton Mifflin publishers at that time, compiled a list of 348 words that first-graders (aged 6–7) should be able to recognize. He asked Theodor Seuss Geisel, an American cartoonist also known as Dr. Seuss, to reduce the list to 250 words and to write an entertaining yet educational book using only those words.

Geisel thought this was impossible, but he accepted the brief and wrote *The Cat in the Hat*, (1957) using only 236 of the words. It had sold close to a million copies by its third year. Geisel managed to one-up himself by writing *Green Eggs and Ham*, which used only 49 words of one syllable, plus the word 'anywhere'.

What this story shows us is that accepting a challenge can be beneficial to our work, and that constraints bring out the best in us. As the case of Dr. Seuss proves, they may even make us surpass ourselves.

Opposite: All 236 words used in *The Cat in the Hat*.

a	fear	jumps	rake	those
about	fell	kicks	ran	thump
after	find	kind	red	thumps
all	fish	kinds	rid	tip
always	fly	kite	run	to
and	for	kites	sad	too
another	fox	know	said	top
any	from	last	sally	toy
are	fun	let	sank	trick
as	funny	like	sat	tricks
asked	game	lit	saw	two
at	games	little	say	up
away	gave	look	see	us
back	get	looked	shake	wall
bad	give	lot	shame	want
ball	go	lots	she	was
be	gone	made	shine	way
bed	good	make	ship	we
bent	got	man	shook	well
bet	gown	mat	should	went
big	had	me	show	were
bit	hall	mess	shut	wet
bite	hand	milk	sit	what
book	hands	mind	so	when
books	has	mother	some	white
bow	hat	mother's	something	who
box	have	my	stand	why
bump	he	near	step	will
bumps	head	net	stop	wish
but	hear	new	string	with
cake	her	no	strings	wood
call	here	not	sun	would
came	high	nothing	sunny	yes
can	him	now	tail	yet
cat	his	of	take	you
cold	hit	oh	tall	your
come	hold	on	tame	
could	home	one	tell	
cup	hook	our	that	
day	hop	out	the	
dear	hops	pack	their	
deep	house	pat	them	
did	how	pick	then	
dish	I	picked	there	
do	if	pink	these	
dots	in	play	they	
down	into	playthings	thing	
fall	is	plop	things	
fan	it	pot	think	
fast	jump	put	this	

'HOW CAN YOU GOVERN A COUNTRY THAT HAS 246 VARIETIES OF CHEESE?'

Charles de Gaulle

Limitations of Medium

WHAT IS MINIMALISM?

Minimalism is often understood as the practice of using very little of everything. But if you think about it more analytically, minimalism is simply the process of applying an extra layer of limitation to a certain medium.

Every medium has its own inherent restrictions. Whether it's on screen or on paper, every design has physical boundaries that we need to work within.

Apple is a great example of this. It limits the number of ports on the sides of its laptops to about six, while other companies might easily have double that. In a generation of 20-button MP3 players, Apple introduced something with four buttons and a wheel that became the most successful portable music device of all time. The iPod and the iPhone have always been noteworthy not because of how much they have, but how little.

Minimalism doesn't just mean using less of everything – it means using a few key things really, really well. In other words, simplify – and intensify.

HOW TO SIMPLIFY AND INTENSIFY

Through simplification, you are able to re-evaluate your priorities. Limiting what you can include will push you to judge which design elements you need, or what physical tools are really important to include. Simplifying begins with a recognition of what is unnecessary.

01

Make a list of all the elements and features of your subject that aren't needed.

02

Start eliminating these unnecessary elements, and continue until you've reached 'minimal functionality'.

03

Organize what remains! Having a system will make things look simpler.

'PERFECTION IS FINALLY ATTAINED NOT WHEN THERE IS NO LONGER ANYTHING TO ADD, BUT WHEN THERE IS NO LONGER ANYTHING TO TAKE AWAY.'

Antoine de Saint-Exupéry

MAXIMUM MEANING MINIMUM MEANS!

The concept of telling a story with the absolute minimum of words is known as 'flash fiction' or 'sudden fiction'. One of the most famous examples is attributed to Ernest Hemingway. It's said that Hemingway bet some friends that he could write an entire story in just six words. Of course, it seemed impossible. Here's how he did it [SEE OPPOSITE]. Who knew that so few words could make up a whole story?

☛ Now it's your turn. Try writing a six-word piece about one of these topics: 'What limitations mean to you'; 'Describe yourself in six words'; 'A résumé of your day'; or if you're in a team: 'What you appreciate about your co-workers'. Here are some useful tips:

▸ Use at least one verb. This story needs action!

▸ Surprise the reader with a twist ending.

▸ Use one strong image to base your story on.

▸ The more specific the topic, the better.

'For sale:
baby shoes, never worn.'

EMBRACING TECHNICAL LIMITATIONS

Mario, of *Super Mario* fame, is probably the best-known video game character, so it might surprise you to know that he had to deal with serious limitations while being created.

Well, not himself, but his designer, Shigeru Miyamoto. Because of the challenges of 8-bit technology back in the 1980s, Miyamoto had to compensate for poor pixel definition.

He gave Mario a large nose (to emphasize the cartoonish character), a moustache (to make a mouth and facial expressions unnecessary), a cap (to overcome the difficulties of animating hair), and a pair of blue overalls (to accentuate his arms in relation to his body).

Mario was basically born out of restrictions. The way he looks and behaves is almost entirely dictated by the visual limitations of the time – and we wouldn't change a thing.

USE YOUR DIGITS!

In the digital age, it becomes more and more important not to rely entirely on computers, especially when it comes to forming creative thoughts.

Sitting at a computer is passive – it stifles your senses and kills your creativity. It also brings out the perfectionist in us – we start editing and deleting ideas before we've even finished forming them!

Work that comes only from the head isn't any good anyway. Watch a great musician play at a concert; watch a great leader give a speech – they are both actively expressing their ideas. If we write something down and feel the pencil on the paper, or shuffle sticky notes around on a mood board, the physical motion kick-starts our brain into thinking.

Use your hands again! Use your digits!*

* Latin: *digitus* = finger

'IF YOU TREAT THE PROBLEMS AS POSSIBILITIES, LIFE WILL START TO DANCE WITH YOU IN THE MOST AMAZING WAYS.'

Martin Villeneuve

Limitations of Skills

MAINTAIN MOMENTUM

We probably all know those meetings with the guy who has one knockout idea after another. It can dent our confidence and stunt our creative momentum.

Instead of killing the momentum with thoughts like 'I can't do it because ...', start with, 'I can do it if ...'

Remember, there are no bad solutions. Keep up the flow of 'I can do it if ...' to maintain a sequence in which one solution leads to another. It keeps the focus on how, not on whether it might be possible. It forces you to find answers rather than seeing barriers, and this approach will motivate you to keep at it, no matter how hard you have to try.

So, to keep up the momentum, stay optimistic, stay on the right track and avoid any negative thoughts that block your focus.

I can do it if . . . .

TEAM UP WITH OTHERS

If you have tried everything and are still stuck because of deficits in your skill set, you have to be open-minded enough to team up with someone who can be your missing link – or your better half.

If you offer them complementary talents, they are more likely to partner with you and help you raise the project to a higher level.

Other people always offer new perspectives and approaches, and also provide an impact you could not have achieved on your own.

By the way, it's always good to hire people who are brighter/funnier/more creative than you, and it's important that you each bring something different to the party. Why would you just hire another you?

$$1 + 1 = 3$$

TRY RANDOM LIMITATIONS

Perhaps you're one of those rare people who possesses skills by the bucketload. It doesn't mean that limitations can't still be valuable to you. Why not impose random rules for yourself? Do it like George Harrison! The lead guitarist of the Beatles opened up a book at random and decided to write a song about whatever words he read first. Harrison saw the words 'gently weeps' and wrote – you guessed it – 'While My Guitar Gently Weeps'.

Composers have been working with limitations to shake things up for a long time. You may have heard of the musical dice game, in which composers literally rolled the dice to choose the order in which (pre-written) bars of music would appear in a piece of music. Mozart himself played the game.

☛ Don't know what colour to choose for one of your designs? Why not play the dice game? Every number of spots is a specific colour; you just have to roll the dice.

☛ Open a magazine at random and use the first picture you see for a collage.

The Beatles
While My Guitar Gently Weeps

* Due to copyright limitations. I had to 'white' out the lyrics.

HARNESS SOMEONE ELSE'S CREATIVITY

Austin Kleon's bestselling book *Newspaper Blackout* (2010) is a collection of poetry made by redacting newspaper articles with a permanent marker, leaving only a few words behind.

Using someone else's property in this way can help galvanize your own skills: you may not be journalistically inclined, but you might just prove to be a damn fine poet.

Indeed, this is not only a great exercise for writers but also for typographers. On the one hand, the words have to make sense, so it's perfect for improving copywriting skills. On the other, you might aim for a good typographic composition of contrasting headline, subhead and body text.

☛ Black out, cut out, do a collage, mix it up – there are definitely some old magazines and books on your shelves that you no longer need.

deathly

little hands

drape

from

the

bodies she

hangs in her living room

a

murals

of

life and death

'THE MORE CONSTRAINTS
ONE IMPOSES, THE MORE
ONE FREES ONESELF
OF THE CHAINS THAT
SHACKLE THE SPIRIT.'

Igor Stravinsky

Limitations of Space

SIZE DOES MATTER!

Michael Johansson is a Swedish artist whose work uses spatial constraints to explore physical objects and spaces.

In what he calls 'real life Tetris', Johansson takes recycled objects, such as suitcases, lockers and storage boxes, and reorganizes them, like a puzzle, to fill a chosen space. What's interesting about Johansson's art is that his starting point is a limitation – he chooses a tight physical framework to work within.

This framework forces Johansson to conduct his creative decision-making in a particular way. The main challenge usually lies in finding the right objects to fit in a certain spot.

It's basically a nice little analogy to the work of a communication designer, who is also trying to make a message fit in a certain medium, whether it's a huge poster or a pocket flyer.

'I ALMOST FEEL THAT THE WORK MAKES ITSELF ONCE I [GET] STARTED.'

Michael Johansson

DECIDE WHAT'S IMPORTANT

When I saw Johansson's work for the first time, it reminded me of the famous Nakagin Capsule Tower in Tokyo, designed by architect Kisho Kurokawa in 1972. The building houses 140 self-contained prefabricated capsules, which measure only 2.5 × 4 metres (8 × 13 feet) with a small window at one end.

Could you imagine living in such a small space? Given the fact that the average European owns around 10,000 things, it is hard to believe that other people on this planet can live with so much less.

We all have too much stuff and it's difficult to recognize what's truly necessary and what's just clutter. We subconsciously acquire more belongings to fill up unused space. But when you're limited in space, you're forced to cut things out. This will make you see the value in your belongings and force you to use them even more industriously. You'll also realize how many things you have that you don't actually need at all!

Get rid of the clutter. A clean mind helps you to focus on the important things again.

DO IT 'LIKE A ROLLING STONE'

How? By making the most of whatever space you're in. Mick Jagger's trademark moves grew out of the fact that in the Rolling Stones' earliest days, the tiny venues in which the band played left almost no room for the singer. Jagger really wanted to engage with the crowd, so he had to develop extravagant moves that worked in confined spaces.

Jagger's bandmate Keith Richards explained in his autobiography, *Life* (2010), how the distinctive dance style came about: 'The spaces were small, which suited us. It suited Mick best of all. Mick's artistry was on display in these small venues ... Give Mick Jagger a stage the size of a table and he could work it better than anybody, except maybe James Brown.'

Jagger turned this limitation into a benefit and evolved his unique dance moves, which became so distinctive and so popular. Limited space could have held him back; instead it made him an even more thrilling frontman.

THE ULTIMATE LIMITATION SCALE

We can always learn from those who have pushed the limits and made it out successfully.

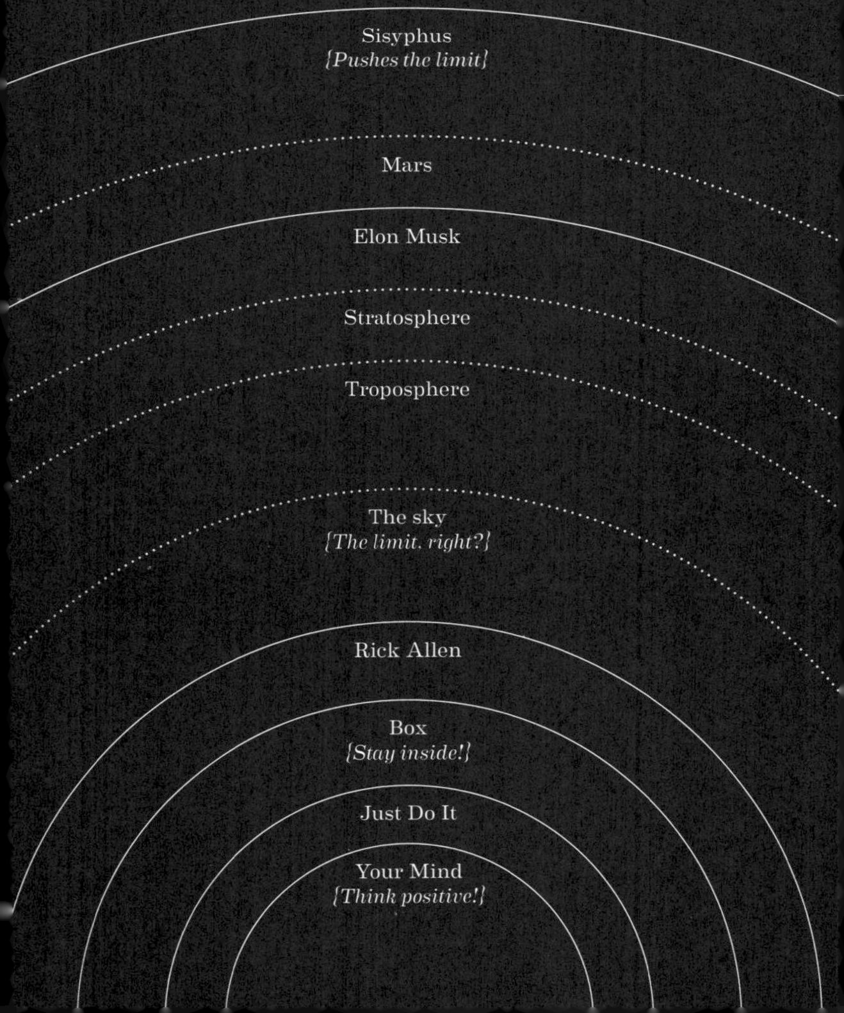
Sisyphus
{Pushes the limit}
Mars
Elon Musk
Stratosphere
Troposphere
The sky
{The limit, right?}
Rick Allen
Box
{Stay inside!}
Just Do It
Your Mind
{Think positive!}

'YOU'VE GOT TO KNOW
YOUR LIMITATIONS ...
I FOUND OUT WHAT MINE
WERE WHEN I WAS
TWELVE. I FOUND OUT
THAT THERE WEREN'T
TOO MANY LIMITATIONS,
IF I DID IT MY WAY.'

Johnny Cash

Final Thoughts

TAKE THE FIRST STEP!

Take the first step. Do it! If you don't know where to begin, start with your limitations. Don't stop because you have limited resources, time, skills, etc. Limitations can seem so insurmountable in the beginning that it's tempting just to give up. It's a form of self-defence.

We all know how the fear of facing something difficult makes us procrastinate the rest of the day. So make the emphasis on 'start' rather than 'complete'.

▸ In the beginning it can be hard to see any potential in limitations. Don't let this lower your ambitions. Instead of seeing yourself as a victim fighting against the limitation, see yourself as a true problem-solver who delights in jumping hurdles.

▸ Once you have dealt with one limitation, you'll feel more confident dealing with others – maintain the momentum. As you spend more time with a problem, you'll see a light at the end of the tunnel and find a way to propel yourself through it.

▶ Finally, you'll see the limitation as an opportunity to explore new kinds of solutions. You'll even be able to increase your ambitions.

WHAT TO DO WITH IMMUTABLE LIMITATIONS

Not all limitations are liberating:

▸ The complete absence of a particular resource must be compensated for or you will immediately start to lower your ambitions.

▸ A repetition of the same limitation(s) won't stimulate creativity; it will just wear you down.

▸ An excess of limitations can demotivate and also paralyse.

Make a list of things that are limiting you and evaluate how easily you can bypass them, let's say from 'No chance' to 'Possible'.

When there is no money at all, *nada*, you will probably have to add more time to come up with a breakthrough idea that is still affordable. Often the trick is to find the right balance between limitations and creating alternatives, especially when you are going to end up capitulating again and again ...

CAPITULATION
CAPITULATION
CAPITULATION
CAPITULATION
CAPITULATION
CAPITULATION
CAPITULATION
CAPITULATION
CAPITULATION
CAPITULATION
CAPITULATION
CAPITULATION
CAPITULATION
CAPITULATION
CAPITULATION
CAPITULATION
CAPITULATION
CAPITULATION
CAPITULATION
CAPITULATION
CAPITULATION
CAPITULATION
CAPITULATION
CAPITULATION

‍ew generation o
and more. They
‍ time in high de
food and have it d
uploading their h
lity on social med

‍mands goes on a
‍oming unreasona
‍wareness of the

‍eems paradoxical,
is beneficial to pro
be more creative
‍w generation wa
‍ble at first sight.

‍ands lead to a con
‍ialized in solving
‍e ourselves to be
ful and more 'insp

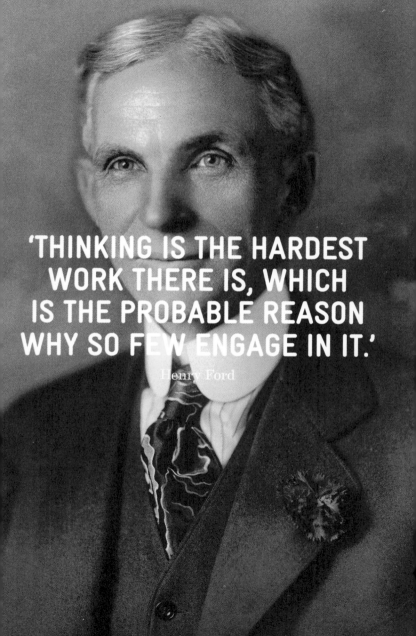

'THINKING IS THE HARDEST WORK THERE IS, WHICH IS THE PROBABLE REASON WHY SO FEW ENGAGE IN IT.'

Henry Ford

LIMITED TO ONLY ONE WORLD

We all live in a world of limited natural resources, yet a mindset of 'bigger, better, faster' prevails. Embracing limitations in our creative lives is a useful lesson that will need to be applied on a much larger scale: we must learn to live with limitations if we want future generations to go on living on this Earth.

'Less is more', a statement often associated with minimalism in architecture, is a premise that has become more important than ever in a world with finite resources. As we look to the future, we will need more people who are capable of turning limitations into possibilities – and who can inspire others to do the same.

This capability is no longer just the business of creatives and designers – it's everyone's business now.

* You and 7.6 billion other people live here as of February 2019.

Picture Credits

15 Vincent van Gogh, *Self Portrait*, 1887. Image courtesy of the Rijksmuseum ¶ **29** Paul Valéry, c.1925, by Henri Manuel ¶ **31** Philippe Starck, Juicy Salif © Alessandro Milani. Alessi ¶ **45** © Happy Person/shutterstock.com ¶ **55** Etching of Pythagoras by Remondini (cropped & coloured) from the Wellcome Collection Library, London (CC BY 4.0) ¶ **61** Billy bookcase, designed by Gillis Lundgren, 1979 © IKEA ¶ **63** Interior view of 'mail box' for purging carbon dioxide from lunar module, 1970 © NASA ¶ **65** Allan Wexler, *I Want to Become Architecture*, 2002 © Ronald Feldman Gallery, New York City ¶ **73** © Nattapon Klinsuwan/shutterstock.com ¶ **75** © Andrey Oleynik/shutterstock.com ¶ **79** David Ogilvy, 1955 © Photo provided by The Ogilvy Group ¶ **83** Lasse Virén, Suomi–Ruotsi-maaottelu Stadionilla, 1980 © Reijo Pasanen (CC BY 4.0) ¶ **95** © marysuperstudio/shutterstock. com ¶ **107** *Murals of Life and Death* © Alice Whitmore, 2014 ¶ **111** Michael Johansson, *Ghost V*, 2011, 2.2×2.2×2 m. © The Flat – Massimo Carasi, Milan ¶ **113** Nakagin capsule tower, Chūō-ku, Japan © Raphael Koh, 2016 (CC BY 1.0) ¶ **115** © Morphart Creation/shutterstock.com ¶ **121** © Channarong Pherngjanda/shutterstock.com ¶ **125** Portrait of Henry Ford (cropped & coloured), 1919, by Fred Hartsook. Source: Library of Congress ¶ **127** *The Blue Marble*, 1972 © NASA/Apollo 17 crew: taken by either Harrison Schmitt or Ron Evans

Bibliography

Robert Poynton, *Do improvise*, The Do Book Company, London, 2013 ¶ Drew Boyd and Jacob Goldenberg, *Inside the Box*, Profile Books, London, 2013 ¶ Adam Morgan and Mark Barden, *A Beautiful Constraint*, Wiley, New Jersey, 2015 ¶ Edward de Bono, *De Bono's Thinking Course*, Pearson Ed., London, 2006 ¶ Keith Richards, *Life*, Phoenix, London, 2011

Thanks

Michael Johansson, Allan Wexler, Zara Larcombe, Katherine Pitt, Brian Piper, Petra Maier and my family.